AIR WAR ARCHIVE

LUFTWAFFE TRAINING AIRCRAFT

THE TRAINING OF GERMANY'S PILOTS AND AIRCREW THROUGH RARE ARCHIVE PHOTOGRAPHS

PREFACE

I have been researching and writing about the Luftwaffe for over 30 years and during this time, have amassed quite a number of photographs. Whilst most of them are of combat aircraft or operational aircrew, I have obtained, both copies and originals, many photos of training units, their men and aircraft. This is understandable as the Luftwaffe's training system was massive and, away from the pressures of the front line, people had more time to take photographs. Whilst this book does not aim to be a definitive or in-depth study of the Luftwaffe's training units and their aircraft, it is intended as a guide of what aircraft were used and a tribute to the instructors and pilots, many of whom did not survive the war.

Chris Goss
January 2019

INTRODUCTION

Following the creation of the Luftwaffe on 1 March 1935, military flying training not only became overt but also massive with a considerable numbers of not just flying schools but of aircraft and aircraft types.

After being inducted to the military, recruits were posted to a Fliegerersätzabteilung (which would later become a Fliegerausbildungsregiment. On successful completion, trainee aircrew were posted to a Fluganwärterkompanie for non-commissioned personnel or Luftkriegsschule for officers. These were essentially a ground school and where pilots were introduced to aircraft. The logbook of one officer cadet shows that he arrived at Luftkriegsschule Dresden Klotzsche on 4 December 1936 after which he was posted to Luftkriegsschule Berlin Gatow where on 21 May 1937 he flew his first flight and his first solo flight was then in an He 72 on 9 June 1937. Later, initial flying training was undertaken by Flugzeugführerschule (A/B) which was then followed by Flugzeugführerschule (C) for advanced training. However, in the case of fighter pilots, they would next be posted to a Jagdfliegervorschule or Jagdfliegerschule. In 1942, the eight Jagdfliegerschule became Jagdgeschwader 101 to Jagdgeschwader 108 and would be augmented by Jagdgeschwader 109 to Jagdgeschwader 112. In the case of our officer cadet, after the award of his pilot's badge, in July 1938 he was posted to the Jagdfliegerschule at Werneuchen to be trained as a fighter pilot and the following month was posted to 9./Jagdgeschwader 132 at Jüterbog-Damm. By means of example, the logbook of a non-commissioned officer shows he first flew with Fliegerausbildungsregiment 42 at Salzwedel on March 1939 and after blind flying training at Prenzlau (still with Fliegerausbildungsregiment 42) he was then posted to Jagdfliegerschule 1 in November 1939 before joining 2 Staffel./Jagdgeschwader 53 the following month.

For pilots selected for other types, bomber pilots would be posted to a Grosse Kampffliegerschule, dive-bomber pilots to a Sturzkampffliegervorschule and reconnaissance pilots to Aufklärungsfliegerschule. In the case of the five Kampffliegerschule, in October 1942 they were re-designated as either Kampfbeobachterschule or Kampfschulegeschwader with the latter becoming Kampfgeschwader 101 the following year.

Following the outbreak of war, even more training was needed. Each bomber and fighter Geschwader would now have its own Ergänzungs or Ausbildungsstaffel or Ergänzungsgruppe which, in the case of bombers, would then be designated IV Gruppe. In the case of fighter pilots, in 1942, the Ergänzungs element went to form Ergänzungsjagdgruppe Ost, Süd and West.

Each aircraft role had its own school as did specialist roles such as Waffenschule, minelaying and torpedo-dropping as well as Beobacher, Bordfunker, Bordmechaniker and Bordschützen schools. There were also blind flying (instrument) schools – our officer cadet (now a Leutnant) attended such a course at Nordhausen between 18 January and 24 February 1940 in order to be a blind flying instructor after which he returned to 1 Staffel/Zerstörergeschwader 76.

As a postscript, the operational careers of both our fighter pilots were short – the officer was shot down and taken prisoner on 15 August 1940 whilst the NCO was shot down and taken prisoner on 5 October 1940.

Opposite: Unteroffizier Willi Ghesla flew Bf 109s with 2. and then 1./Jagdgeschwader 53. He was shot down and taken prisoner over Kent on 5 October 1940. He had previously trained at Fliegerausbildungsregiment 42 Salzwedel and then Jagdfliegerschule 1 at Werneuchen.

Below: Leutnant Hans-Ulrich Kettling flew Bf 110s with 1./Zerstörergeschwader 76. He was shot down and taken prisoner over County Durham on 15 August 1940. He had trained at Luftkriegsschule Berlin Gatow then Jagdfliegerschule Werneuchen before being posted to 9./Jagdgeschwader 132.

Trainee pilots from Fliegerausbildungsregiment 42 (note the lack of pilot's badges) and their instructor (kneeling centre with pilot's badge – believed to be Unteroffizier Lauerer), Wunsdorf June 1939. Note that nearly all share the same rank as the instructor. Those who successfully completed training would find themselves flying operationally from early 1940 and many, like Unteroffizier Willi Ghesla kneeling right, would be captured or killed before the year was out.

GLOSSARY

Aufklärer	Reconnaissance
Ausbildung	Training
Blindflug	Blind flying
Bordfunker	Radio Operator
Beobachter	Observer
Bordmechaniker	Flight Engineer
Bordschütze	Air Gunner
Do	Dornier
Ergänzungs	Training
Fähnrich	Officer Cadet
Feindflug	Operational flight
Feldwebel	Flight Sergeant
Fern	Long range
Flieger	Aircraftman
Fliegerersatzabteilung	Basic training unit
Fliegerausbildungsregiment	Same as Fliegerersatzabteilung
Fluzeugführer	Pilot
Fluzeugführerschule (A/B)	Elementary flying training school
Fluzeugführerschule (C)	Advanced flying training school
Führer	Leader
Funker	Radio
Gefreiter	Leading Aircraftman
Geschwader	Group consisting three Gruppen commanded by a Geschwader Kommodore
Grosse Kampffliegerschule	Bomber school
Gruppe	Wing consisting three Staffeln; commanded by a Gruppen Kommandeur. Gruppe number denoted by Roman numerals (e.g. II).
Hauptmann	Flight Lieutenant/Captain
He	Heinkel

Jabo	Fighter-bomber
Jagd	Fighter
Ju	Junkers
Kampf	Bomber
Kette	Three-aircraft tactical formation similar to RAF vic
Lehrgeschwader	Technical Development Flying Group
Leutnant	Pilot Officer/2nd Lieutenant
Luftflotte	Air Fleet
Luftkriegsschule	Officer training school
Major	Squadron Leader/Major
Me	Messerschmitt (used by RAF)
Nachtjagdgeschwader	Night fighter Group
Nachtrichten	Signals
Oberfeldwebel	Warrant Officer
Obergefreiter	Senior Aircraftman/Corporal
Oberleutnant	Flying Officer/1st Lieutenant
Oberst	Group Captain/Colonel
Oberstleutnant	Wing Commander/Lieutenant Colonel
Reichsluftfahrtministerium	Germany Air Ministry
Reichsmarschall	Marshal of the Air Force
Rotte	Two-aircraft tactical formation; two Rotten made a Schwarm; commanded by a Rottenführer
Rottenflieger	Wingman
Schlacht	Ground attack
Schule	School
Schwarm	Four aircraft tactical formation commanded by a Schwarm Führer
Seenotflug	Air-Sea rescue
Stab	Staff or HQ; formation in which Gruppen Kommandeur and Geschwader Kommodore flew.
Stabsfeldwebel	Senior Warrant Officer
Staffel	Squadron (twelve aircraft); commanded by a Staffel Kapitän. Staffel number denoted by Arabic numerals (e.g. 2)
stammkennzeichen	Factory codes
Sturzkampfflugzeug (Stuka)	Dive bomber
Unteroffizier	Sergeant
Vorschule	Pre-school
Waffenschule	Weapons school
werk nummer	Serial number
Zerstörer (Z)	Destroyer/Heavy fighter

ARADO

An Arado Ar 66 photographed at Schule/Fliegerausbildungsregiment 13 between April and May 1940 by Fähnrich Leopold Wenger. Fliegerausbildungsregiment 13 was based at Pilsen but also used the airstrip at Klattau. Wenger would complete training and was posted to I./Jagdgeschwader 2 in late 1941 but after that became a Jabo (fighter-bomber) pilot with 10./Jagdgeschwader 2. He would be awarded the Knight's Cross but was killed in action on 10 April 1945.

An Ar 66 seen at an unknown flying school. The date would appear to be spring/summer 1939.

Opposite above: Ar 66 C werk nummer 1239 DK+OG of Schule/Fliegerausbildungsregiment 13 photographed April–May 1940. Records prove it was still there on 28 November 1940 but was destroyed in an accident at Karlsbad on 3 August 1941 in which the pilot, Gefreiter Hans Dürr, was killed.

Opposite below: An Ar 66 coded WL, this code being officially used by Luftwaffe training aircraft from January to October 1939 having replaced the five letter/number combination. It was replaced by the four-letter stammkennzeichen.

An Ar 66 BO+DF of *Luftkriegsschule* 4, Fürstenfeldbruck. This aircraft was recorded as being there on 18 June 1941. The photograph was taken by Fähnrich Siegfried Storsberg who would remain as an instructor at *Jagdfliegerschule* 1 Werneuchen after which he joined Jagdgeschwader 26 in late 1942. He would then specialize as a Jabo pilot and survived the war.

Ar 66 DK+JM and BO+DF of Luftkriegsschule 4, 1941. The former was first recorded at this unit on 9 September 1940 and was still there on 8 August 1941. It next appears on the inventory of 1./Schlachtgeschwader 111, which was based at Stubendorf and Ludwigslust, from December 1943 to 26 July 1944.

Opposite above: Ar 66s of an unidentified flying school being refuelled at a German or Austrian airfield.

Opposite below: This Ar 66 C carries a civilian code as it is being used for private flying. Most civil aircraft were taken up by the Luftwaffe as the war approached.

Ar 66 RQ+NC of Luftkriegsschule 4, 1941. This aircraft was recorded as being with Luftkriegsschule 4 from 28 May 1941 to 8 November 1943. Its final fate is not known.

D-IZOF

40 2 624

Two Ar 68s of an unidentified unit having come to grief, presumably due to the boggy condition of the airfield. Of interest are the roundels behind the wing and fuselage crosses which would indicate the aircraft have been taking part in a pre-war exercise.

Opposite above: Ar 68s of Jagdfliegerschule Werneuchen, 1938. The full code of the nearest aircraft would be S2+G24 which denotes Schule; Luftkreis 2; Flight G; aircraft 24. The third aircraft is S2+M15. Such codes first appear in the logbook of Leutnant Hans-Ulrich Kettling in December 1937.

Opposite below: Mechanics of Jagdfliegerschule Werneuchen working on a Ar 68 in the field, summer 1938.

Opposite above: Debrief or a posed photograph in front of an Ar 68 of Jagdfliegerschule Werneuchen, summer 1938.

Opposite below: Starting up an Ar 68 of Jagdfliegerschule Werneuchen, summer 1938.

A pilot about to climb into his Ar 68, Jagdfliegerschule Werneuchen, summer 1938. Note the Fw 56s in the background.

2

Opposite above: Taken later in the war, this Ar 68, in addition to darker camouflage, has what appears to be a yellow fuselage band. It is possible that the stammkennzeichen is DB+NY.

Opposite below: Note the second letter of the stammkennzeichen on the fuselage band of this Ar 68.

Taken at an unidentified flying school later in the war, this Ar 68 sports much darker camouflage.

6

87

Designed as a lightweight single-seat advanced fighter trainer, the Ar 76 was found to be inferior to the Fw 56 and as a result, very few were made. This example has civil markings and note the Arado company badge above the wheel spat.

Opposite above: The Ar 68 was intended as a replacement for the He 51 but by 1939 was being used predominantly as a trainer. This aircraft is coloured light grey and has a white 6, indicating it to be a 1 Staffel aircraft possibly from a front-line unit.

Opposite below: Rearming the machine guns of an Ar 68 of Jagdfliegerschule Werneuchen, summer 1938. The triangle 87 denotes the fuel octane number.

Opposite above: Oberfeldwebel Weber at the controls of an Ar 96 of 3./Jagdfliegerschule 4 at Fürth. This school would become Jagdgeschwader 104 in 1943. The badge of Jagdfliegerschule 4 is a black winged arrow on a white triangle in a red shield on the top of which are the words 'Jagdfl-Schule 4' in black in a blue box. The pilot who took this photo was Gefreiter Hans Derksen who would be posted to 7./Jagdgeschwader 302 and was killed in an accident on the night of 25 November 1943 when his Bf 109 G-6, werk nummer 410142, crashed at Wehnen near his base at Oldenburg.

Opposite below: Ar 96s of Jagdfliegerschule 5 on a training flight from Guyancourt to Le Havre, August 1941.

Ar 76 werk nummer 752 CN+HG of Schule/Fliegerausbildungsregiment 82 at Cottbus. This aircraft was first recorded at this school on 11 January 1940 and was still there on 4 May 1941. Its final fate is not known.

262
254

73
77

Ar 96 werk nummer 1004 BH+AY was first reported at Schule/Fliegerausbildungsregiment 14, Pilsen on 8 February 1940. In June 1940 it was at Schule/Fliegerausbildungsregiment 24 and then on 12 May 1941 at Schule/Fliegerausbildungsregiment 72, Markersdorf where presumably this photograph was taken by Gefreiter Werner Schammert. Schammert would eventually join 10./Jagdgeschwader 26 and was shot down by anti-aircraft fire attacking RAF Manston in Kent on 10 October 1942; he managed to bale out and was captured.

Opposite above: Ar 96 werk nummer 4102 DE+NB first served with Nachtjagdschule 1 at Schleissheim and then I./Nachtjagdgeschwader 101. On 15 January 15 1942, it suffered 40 per cent damage when it had engine failure and force-landed near Hochbrück.

Opposite below: DE+NB was repaired after its January 1942 accident only to be totally destroyed in a crash at Schwaig on 9 May 1943. Feldwebel Kurt Martin was killed and Gefreiter Fritz Wendel injured. It was still with I./Nachtjagdgeschwader 101 at the time of its crash. Note the yellow letter A on the fuselage.

73
70

Ar 196 A-2s and, third aircraft in, an He 114 of 4.(Ergänzungs)/Bordfliegergruppe 196, possibly taken at Thisted, Denmark. This unit was also known as 4./Bordflieger Ergänzungsstaffel but was only in existence from February to April 1941 before becoming 2./Aufklärungsgruppe 125 (See). Ar 196 A-2s also flew with 3./Bordflieger Ergänzungsgruppe (See). The badge show has two grey seahorses on a blue shield.

Opposite above: An Ar 96 presumably of Jagdfliegerschule 1. Note the werk nummer on both the rudder and cowling and the first two letters of the stammkennzeichen BS+.

Opposite below: Another view of Ar 96s of Jagdfliegerschule 5 flying from Guyancourt in February 1942. As Allied air superiority increased, such flights were carried out further away from the front line.

Ar 196s of 4.(Ergänzungs)/Bordfliegergruppe 196 carrying out tail-chasing. This floatplane proved itself to be a very capable and manoeuvrable aircraft and was popular to fly.

BÜCKER

Bü 131 'Jungmann' werk nummer 4560 seen at Luftkriegsschule 4, Fürstenfeldbruck. At the controls is Fähnrich Ulrich Laubis, who would be shot down and taken prisoner while serving with 3./Kampfgeschwader 77 on 23 June 1944.

D-ENBA

The Bü 181 'Bestmann' was another successful Bücker trainer manufactured in the thousands. This one is being operated by Flugzeugführerschule A10, formerly Flugzeugführerschule (See) Warnemünde/ Flugzeugführerschule (See) 1 and Flugzeugführerschule A/B 10, towards the end of the war.

Opposite above: Bücker publicity photo of Bü 131 D-ENBA. Note the company name on the cowling. In recent times, the civilian serial D-ENBA has been assigned to a Cessna 205 operating out of Essen-Mülheim airfield.

Opposite below: The Bü 133 'Jungmeister' first flew in 1935 and proved to be a first-class aerobatics platform and was the chosen aircraft of the Luftwaffe's aerobatics team. With the code YR, this aircraft is an export variant for Romania.

The first flight of Fähnrich Friedrich Jirmann on 31 October 1941 in a Bü 131 of Luftkriegsschule 3, Werder/Havel. Jirmann later joined 13./Kampfgeschwader 2 in October 1943 flying the Me 410, this unit then becoming 5./Kampfgeschwader 51. He was wounded on 25 June 1944 when he was shot down, probably by a Mosquito of 488 Squadron. He was still with Kampfgeschwader 51 at the end of the war, training to fly the Me 262.

Fähnrich Manfred Knirsch at the controls of a Bü 131 of Luftkriegsschule 3. He was later promoted to Leutnant and was last heard of with Stukageschwader 101 in 1943.

DORNIER

Opposite above: Do 17 F werk nummer 1032 DA+NT is first recorded as being with Aufklärungsschule 1 at Grossenhain where it suffered 40 per cent damage on 5 September 1940. It then served with Flugzeugführerschule (C) 6 at Burg and Kolberg June 1941 to May 1942 and was last recorded with the Erprobungsstelle (Test and Evaluation Unit) Travemünde in May 1943.

Opposite below: This Do 17 E-1 of Flugzeugführerschule (C) 16 suffered a taxiing accident. The owl badge confirms the unit.

Below: This Do 17 E-1 werk nummer 3083 TE+LN served with Flugzeugführerschule (C) 16 which was formed at Burg/Magdeburg in May 1940 where it is presumed that this is where the accident occurred. After repair, it was then transferred to the Air Force of the Independent State of Croatia (ZNDH) in April 1943 where it served with 8 zrakoplovno jato (air force squadron) and was written off in an accident near Sisak on 17 August 1944.

The Do 17 Z proved itself to be good, if later vulnerable, in low-level attacks. These aircraft of an unidentified unit are practicing low-level formation flying. The furthest aircraft still has a stammkennzeichen as opposed to unit codes and both aircraft have white spinners.

Opposite above: Although it carries the markings of Kampfgeschwader 51, this photograph was taken by Unteroffizier Günther Unger whilst at II./Grosse Kampffliegerschule 2 at Bad Vöslau near Vienna, autumn 1939. Unger later joined 9./Kampfgeschwader 76, was shot down into the Channel after having been damaged by a Hurricane of 111 Sqn on 18 August 1940 (where he and two of his crew were rescued) and then shot down by anti-aircraft fire on 12 March 1941, he and his crew all being captured.

Opposite below: As the war progressed, the Do 17 was reduced to secondary roles in addition to training. This Do 17 E is towing a DFS 230 glider coded CB+ZB either on trials or training for airborne operations, something the Do 17 was still doing in 1945.

Opposite above: Grosse Kampffliegerschule 2 did not get the Do 17 Z until mid- to late 1941 when the operational Do 17 Z units converted to other types. It would appear aircraft wore stammkennzeichen. This photo was taken at Hörsching and clearly shows the unit badge and vertical band.

Opposite below: The nearest aircraft served with Grosse Kampffliegerschule 1 at Tutow and ultimately with Flugzeugführerschule (C) 4 at airfields in the Niederschlesien region. Its ultimate fate is not known. Note the mix of camouflage and the fuselage band on the front aircraft.

Though hard to discern, this is a Do 17 Z of Grosse Kampffliegerschule 1. The vertical nose band appears to be peculiar to this unit whilst the badge is a quartered black-and-white shield with various symbols including a winged bomb and propeller, lightning bolts and arrows.

The Do 17 Z was still being used for training in 1944. This aircraft is from Flugzeugführerschule (C) 5 at Anklam and was photographed in April 1944. Flugzeugführerschule (C) 5 disbanded in July 1944.

The Do 17s of Kampfgeschwader 2 were replaced by the Do 217 commencing spring 1941. This shows a Do 217 E-4 coded U5+CB of Stab I./Kampfgeschwader 2 flown by Oberleutnant Karl von Manowarda on a training flight from Cognac in western France on 19 June 1942. Von Manowarda was shot down and taken prisoner on 15 May 1944 flying with 1./Kampfgeschwader 6.

FOCKE-WULF

Fw 44 werk nummer 1784 BB+EM was first reported with Schule/Fliegerausbildungsregiment 71 in March 1940 but subsequently served with Luftkriegsschule 4 from at least February 1941 to 30 May 1944.

Known as the 'Stieglitz' or Goldfinch, the Fw 44 first flew in 1932 and a number still fly today.

The Fw 44 was popular as a civil sports plane. Most were taken up by the Luftwaffe at the start of the war.

Opposite above: Fw 44 J werk nummer 2615 CM+HS was first recorded with Schule/Fliegerausbildungsregiment 82 from May 1940 to September 1941 but then in May 1942 it was flying with the tactical reconnaissance unit 1 Staffel (Heer)/Aufklärungsgruppe 12, a Fw 189 unit operating over the Soviet Union, presumably as a training or communications aircraft.

Opposite below: Photographed by Fähnrich Leopold Wenger at Cham, Bavaria on 25 June 1940, this Fw 56 A-1 was with Schule/Fliegerausbildungsregiment 13. The Fw 56 carried the designation 'Stösser' or Goshawk.

Fw 44 PT+NF is first recorded as being with Schule/Fliegerausbildungsregiment 24 in Olmütz at the end of January 1940 but was then with Schule/Fliegerausbildungsregiment 13 in Chiesch at the end of April 1941. Its final fate is not known.

2615
CM
2615

AP

Opposite above: Fw 56 A-1 werk nummer 2501 CT+BG photographed at Cham, 25 June 1940 whilst with Schule/Fliegerausbildungsregiment 13. Initially this aircraft was operated by the Austrian Air Force with Jagdstaffel 1 but after the 1938 Anschluss was operated by Flugbereitschaft des Kommandierenden Generals in Österreich. It then flew with Schule/Fliegerausbildungsregiment 13 until December 1940 and in October 1941 was with Luftzeugamt Liegnitz who delivered it to Flugzeugführerschule (A/B) 113 with which unit it operated until 27 May 1942. It was eventually lost in an accident with 1./Jagdgeschwader 104 on 30 October 30 1943 when it collided with a Fw 56 werk nummer 2440 near Bamberg, its pilot Unteroffizier Karl Gerstengabel being injured.

Opposite below: Fw 56 VB + AH was first recorded with Schule/Fliegerausbildungsregiment 13 at Pilsen in October 1940 and was still there in July 1941. It was then with Flugzeugführerschule (A/B) 13 and recorded there on April and May 1943 after which nothing more is recorded. Note the Focke-Wulf badge below the cockpit.

D-IGUA is either being operated by Luftkriegsschule Berlin-Gatow or Jagdfliegerschule Werneuchen in 1937–8.

T BG

VB AH

2448
VB+AH

The Fw 58 was named 'Weihe' or Harrier, similar to all other of Focke-Wulf's aircraft. This is with Schule/Fliegerausbildungsregiment 13 at Pilsen in July 1940.

Opposite above: VB+AF clearly showing its werk nummer. It would appear that the rudder has been over-painted in white.

Opposite below: Although the markings are not visible, this Fw 58 is with Schule/Fliegerausbildungsregiment 13 at Pilsen in July 1940.

Fw 189 A-0 BQ+AU seen at Holzweiler, winter 1939–40. The aircraft, named 'Uhu' or Eagle Owl, was being introduced to service with 9.(Heer)/Lehrgeschwader 2 which also carried out initial training.

Opposite above: Photographed with Luftkriegsschule 4 at Fürstenfeldbruck, this is a Fw 58 C-2 werk nummer 3611 CB+FN. The date of the crash is unknown but this aircraft was recorded with Luftkriegsschule 4 from February to July 1941 and was later with Flugzeugführerschule (A/B) 122 in March 1942.

Opposite below: A busy scene at Luftkriegsschule 4 at Fürstenfeldbruck in 1941 with an unidentified Fw 58 about to take off.

Taken in March 1940, training on this new aircraft continued at Holzweiler.

Unidentified ground crew member, 9.(Heer)/Lehrgeschwader 2, Erkelenz, winter 1939–40.

Unteroffizier Wolfgang Gerecke (right) getting to grips with the new plane, March 1940. Gerecke was one of the first pilots to fly the aircraft and apparently survived the war.

Operational training did result in losses. On 16 May 1940, BQ+AT was shot down by Hurricanes of 79 Squadron and crashed near Ramillies-Offus, killing Unteroffizier Heinz Schmitz (Fluzeugführer), Wachtmeister Klaus Seehase (Beobachter) and Gefreiter Hans Kaven (Bordschütze). The Fw 189 would then operate successfully over the Soviet Union starting from the end of 1941.

2./Nahauklärungsgruppe 13 was formed at Jüterbog-Damm flying the Fw 190, formed from parts of Aufklärungsgruppe 13. Initial training on the 'Würger' (Butcher Bird) was by the Aufklärungs Lehr und Erprobungsstaffel and was completed on 6 October 1942. In mid-December 1942, it moved to western France to operate from St Brieuc, commencing in February 1943.

DT FO

Werner Schammert climbing into a Fw 190 A coded White 18 of Jagdgruppe West, Cazaux, 1942. He would be shot down and taken prisoner on 10 October 1942.

Opposite above: Unteroffizer Heinz Ehrhardt converted to the Fw 190 and would fly the aircraft in the Jabo role. Here he is undergoing training. After posting to 2./ Schnellkampfgeschwader 10, he would land his Fw 190 in error at RAF Manston on 29 May 1943 during an operational night mission.

Opposite below: An earlier Jabo pilot was Unteroffizier Werner Schammert who is believed to have joined 10./Jagdgeschwader 26 in the latter half of 1942 from Jagdgruppe West where this photograph was taken.

One of a number of spectacular training accidents for Jagdgruppe West was this Fw 190 A-3 Red 21.

Damage to Red 23 appears light so any record of the date or pilot would be hard to find.

Opposite above: Fähnrich Helmut Wenk climbing into the cockpit of werk nummer 5381, Cognac, May 1943. The following month he would be posted to 6./Schnellkampfgeschwader 10 and after flying one mission over the UK, moved with his unit to the Mediterranean.

Opposite below: Furthest from the camera is Fw 200 A-03/S3 werk nummer 0074 coded F8+EU of Ergänzungs Staffel./Kampfgeschwader 40 which was used for resupply and crew training. It was formerly an aircraft of Deutsches Luft Hansa and coded D-ARHW.

By 1943, Jabo training was more formalized. This is a Fw 190 A-3, werk nummer 5381 White 7 of Ergänzungs Staffel/Schnellkampfgeschwader 10 photographed at Cognac in May 1943. This aircraft suffered engine failure on a training flight on 4 June 1943 and crashed 4km north of Bordeaux at 1235hrs, the pilot baling out without injury.

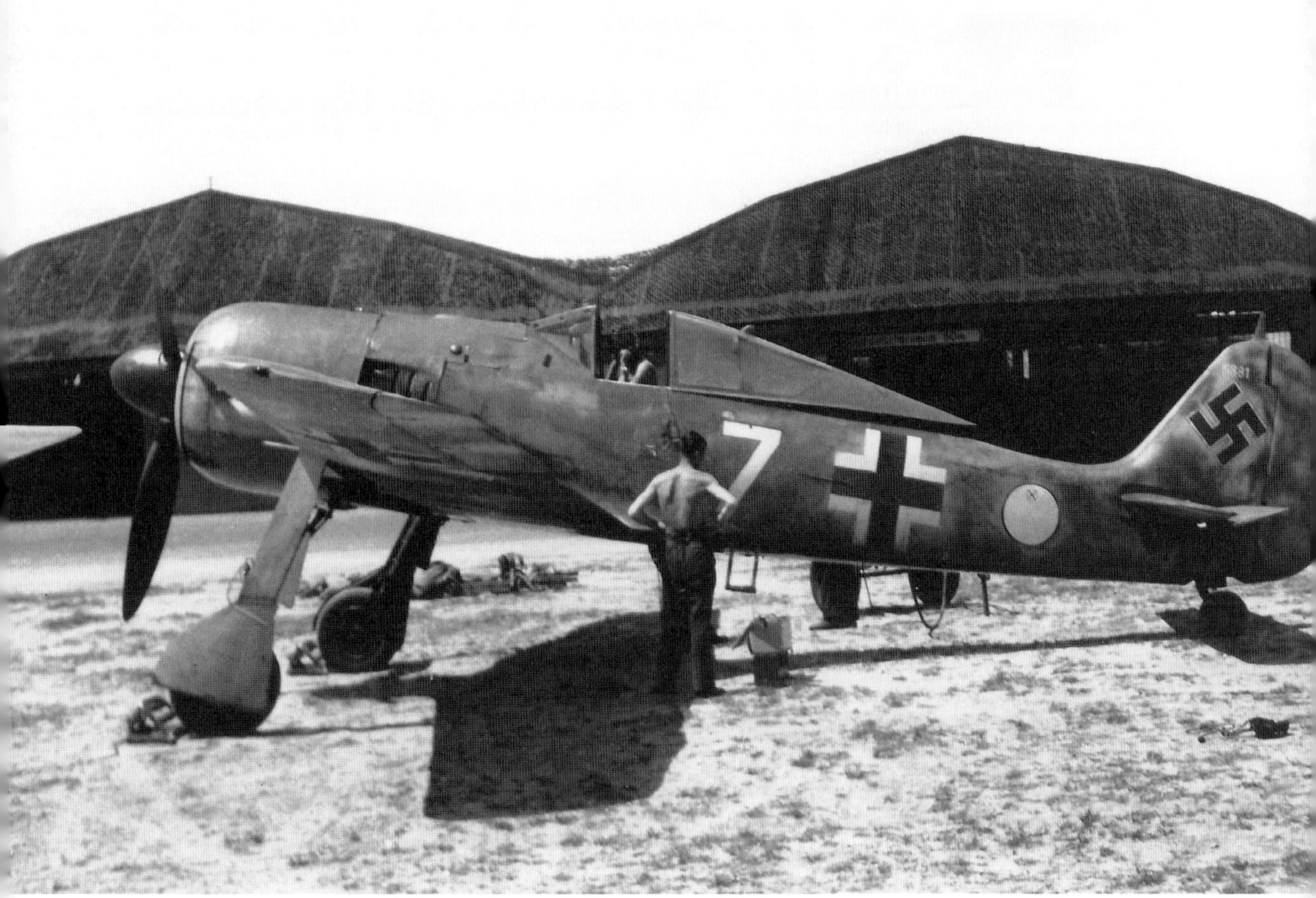

Opposite: A close-up of the tail of F8+BW showing its impressive war record. Sitting on the motorcycle is Hauptmann Hans-Jürgen Willers who commanded 11./Kampfgeschwader 40 in 1942, one of the Staffel responsible for Condor crew training.

This Fw 200 C-2 werk nummer 0016 F8+BW of IV./Kampfgeschwader 40 was used for crew training, having been retired from front-line service at the end of 1941.

Another aircraft retired from front-line service was this Fw 200 C-3 SG+KM of Blindflugschule 6. Its tail also carried evidence of its missions and successes.

Blindflugschule 6 operated this sole Fw 200 for instrument flying training from Wesendorf. The unit's badge was a black and white cow on a circle of red and orange quarters.

GOTHA

A Go 145 of Schule/Fliegerausbildungsregiment 13, Klattau, April–May 1940. The tail to the right belongs to an Ar 66.

An unidentified pilot about to go solo in a Go 145.

Photographed at Luftkriegsschule 4, Fürstenfeldbruck, Go 145 KO+AM was recorded at Luftkriegsschule 1 at Dresden-Heller at the start of July 1941. Note the Fw 58 coded CF+AG in the background. This aircraft served with Schule/Fliegerausbildungsregiment 82 from February to September 1940. It then is recorded at Aufklärungsschule 1 at Grossenhain from the start of September 1941 to May 1942. It is then recorded at Grosse Kampffliegerschule Grossenhain (?) in May 1942, then Flugzeugführerschule (C) from 18 March to September 1943, Flugzeugführerschule (B) 37 in November 1943 and Luftkriegsschule 4 in May 1944.

A much darker-camouflaged Go 145 of either Luftkriegsschule 4 or Jagdfliegerschule 1. The werk nummer is believed to be 1385.

HEINKEL

A He 42B of Flugzeugführerschule (See) coded D-ILHA photographed before the war. This aircraft type was all but obsolete at the outbreak of war.

Opposite above: The He 45 was also obsolete at the outbreak of war but was still used by training units, as KE+AT shows.

Opposite below: Photographed with 3 Staffel (Fern)/Aufklärungsgruppe 123 at Grossenhain in 1936, this unit would re-equip with the Do 17 and these He 45 Cs would become trainers or be scrapped. The code on the middle aircraft is 50+D13.

Flugzeugführerschule (See) was formed at Warnemünde in 1935 and eventually became Flugzeugführerschule A/B 10 at the end of 1940. Before the war, there was also a Flugzeugführerschule (See) 2 at Pütnitz and Flugzeugführerschule (See) 3 at Parow. This He 42 was photographed in 1937.

KE

Opposite above: The He 50 was actively used as a trainer before the war.

Opposite below: Some He 50s were still being used as trainers as late as 1943. Unfortunately the full code of this aircraft cannot be discerned.

The He 46 was another short-lived operational aircraft. This one is from Aufklärungsgruppe (Fern) 122.

Early He 51s in civilian markings.

Opposite above: A popular fighter trainer was the He 51. The full code is S2+J89 and it is seen at Jagdfliegerschule Werneuchen in 1938.

Opposite below: This He 51 had a long career. First registered as D-IGYA in March 1936, it eventually acquired the code TR+HT and werk nummer 1104. It was then with II./Stukaschule 2 in September 1940 and then Flugzeugführerschule (B) 43 where it suffered 30 per cent damage at Crailsheim on 13 November 1941. It was still at the same unit in December 1943 but then suffered 25 per cent damage on 20 January 1944 at Mannheim-Sandhofen whilst with Jagdgeschwader 106.

Refuelling an He 51 of Jagdfliegerschule Werneuchen, summer 1938. The full code is S2+J53.

He 51s of Jagdfliegerschule Werneuchen practicing formation flying. Note the auxiliary fuel tank on the middle aircraft.

The He 72 was known as the 'Kadett'. This aircraft belongs to Flugzeugführerschule (A/B) 72 at Neudorf-Oppeln.

Opposite above: Before the war, the He 59 was used as an armed reconnaissance aircraft but by the outbreak of war, it had been relegated to air-sea rescue duties and training. This is an early He 59 B.

Opposite below: Despite a promising pre-war career as a reconnaissance aircraft, the He 70 was used in the training and communications roles during the war. This aircraft served with Luftkriegsschule 4 at Fürstenfeldbruck/Bad Wörrishofen.

D-EFYO

An He 111 J of Flugzeugführerschule (C) 8 at Wiener-Neustadt. The aircraft carries on the nose the school's badge of a three-leaf clover. In the background is a mixture of aircraft – nearest is a Klemm L25 and in the distance Ju 52s.

Opposite above: An He 72 B-1 wearing pre-war markings.

Opposite below: An early photograph of an He 72; note the name 'Heinkel Kadett' behind the engine.

Opposite above: A close-up view of the He 111 J of Flugzeugführerschule (C) 8 reveals the unit badge.

Opposite below: This He 111 J werk nummer 5057 of Grosse Kampffliegerschule 5 based at Parow in eastern Germany crash-landed at Bamberg due to engine failure on 7 June 1942.

Another scene at Flugzeugführerschule (C) 8. To the right appears to be an He 111 E and to the left, an He 70, both of which are waiting for permission to take off.

He 111 H-1, werk nummer 5101 coded 6N+CH of 1./Kampfgeschwader 100. Flown by Oberfeldwebel Paul Wierbitzky, it suffered engine failure on 20 February 1941 whilst on a training flight and crash-landed at Lüneberg.

Opposite above: The He 111 J was designed following a Kriegsmarine requirement for a torpedo and mine-carrying version of the He 111. When the project was dropped, production continued with the He 111 J mainly serving in training schools. This crew would ultimately fly the Fw 200.

Opposite below: The identity of this pre-war He 111 is unknown but in addition to the oversized wing crosses, the aircraft code is also repeated on the upper wing surfaces outside the crosses.

5101

An unidentified crew in front of an old, unarmed He 111 H, June 1944. Note the bombsight has also been removed.

Opposite above: Kampfgeschwader 100 was a specialist pathfinder unit, hence the additional aerials for the X Gerät navigation system.

Opposite below: This aircraft suffered engine failure again on 10 August 10 1941 at Schwäbisch-Hall, this time suffering 50 per cent damage. By now the Wierbitzky crew had been shot down during an attack on Chatham in Kent on 14 June 1941 and all taken prisoner.

Opposite above: This is believed to be an He 111 H-6/T. This variant was a purpose-built torpedo bomber able to carry two LT F5b torpedoes. The two-tone torpedoes indicate this aircraft is being used for training or trials.

Opposite below: For maritime operations, some He 111 Hs were fitted with FuG 200 Hohentwiel surface-search radar. Note the 20mm MG FF cannon in the nose and the factory code starting GJ+. The lack of unit codes, the civilian mechanics and the pristine nature of this aircraft would indicate that it is being used for trials or training.

This aircraft is believed to be He 111 H-5 BK+CO which should have been werk nummer 3891. This photo is believed to have been taken at the Grossenbrode Waffenschule on the Baltic coast where torpedo training was carried out.

Low-level training over northern Germany for He 111 H-16s of 9./Kampfgeschwader 53, the aircraft in view being coded A1+JT. This unit was in the throes of training for missions launching under-slung V-1s against mainland Britain.

One of the first He 177 prototypes. Although this aircraft first flew in November 1939, due to development problems and then crew training, the He 177 did not carry out its first offensive mission until November 1943.

A rare air-to-air shot of a He 177 A of IV./Kampfgeschwader 40, the Gruppe responsible for He 177 crew training. The numerals on the rudder show that this was a training aircraft.

Three crew members of a He 177. All would be posted to 1./Kampfgeschwader 40 after training but would be shot down on 11 June 1944; the two on the left were captured, the one the right killed. It is assumed that the letter O is the aircraft individual letter but the badge below it is unknown.

HENSCHEL

Originally designed as a ground-attack aircraft, Hs 123 S2+RO is seen here being used as a trainer at Jagdfliegerschule Werneuchen, summer 1938.

Opposite above: S2+R24 of Jagdfliegerschule Werneuchen has a distinctive splinter camouflage.

Opposite below: Five Hs 123s of Jagdfliegerschule Werneuchen, summer 1938.

Visible on the Jagdfliegerschule Wernecuhen Hs 123 is the auxiliary fuel tank, machine guns on top of the cowling and the Junkers-manufactured propellers.

S2
R24

JUNKERS

There are eight Ju W34hau visible in this photograph. The unit is believed to have been Schule/ Fliegerausbildungsregiment 82 at Cottbus.

Working on the engine of a W34hau, Cottbus 1942.

Opposite above: The size of the W34hau made it ideal as a trainer, especially for bomber crews.

Opposite below: Manpower is required to right this W34hi at Cottbus.

Work done, the cowling is back on.

An earlier accident of a W34hau of Luftkriegsschule 4 taken at Fürstenfeldbruck.

Opposite above: Same aircraft needing even more manpower. Note the last two letters of the stammkennzeichen painted over a previous code.

Opposite below: Fähnrich Kurt Becker in a W34 of Luftkriegsschule 4, Bad Worrishöfen Summer 1941. Becker would eventually fly Ju 88 torpedo bombers with I./Kampfgeschwader 77 and I./Kampfgeschwader 26.

Opposite above: Working on a W34hau of Luftkriegsschule 4, Bad Worrishöfen.

Opposite below: Pupils posing on a W34hau of Luftkriegsschule 3. Note the over-sized painting of the werk nummer 924.

Fähnrich Friedrich Jirman posing in front of a W34hau werk nummer 924 of Luftkriegsschule 3, Borkheide, April 1942.

Opposite above: Photographed in 1943, this W34hau has a fuselage band underneath the first letters of its stammkennzeichen. Note how much darker the camouflage has now become.

Opposite below: The original owner of this photograph which shows a W34 from an unidentified unit was Unteroffizier Engelberg Schall. He was a Bordfunker with 3./Stukageschwader 151 and was killed on 9 July 1943 at Ostrice in Croatia. He and others from his unit were trying to recover the bodies of his Gruppen Kommandeur, Hauptmann Armin Thiede, and seven others who had been killed in the crash of a DFS 230 glider, when they were attacked by partisans. In addition to those killed in the crash, another thirteen were killed by partisans.

More posing but this time werk nummer 1473, Wien-Aspern, 3 April 1942.

A pre-war training accident. Ju 52 54+S39 on the strength of III./Kampfgeschwader 255 crashed on 5 November 1937.

Opposite above: A W34hau with the first letters of its *stammkennzeichen* NG+, *Flugzeugführerschule* (AB) 116, Neudorf-Oppeln.

Opposite below: W34hau CA+FZ was werk nummer 3279 of Luftkriegsschule 4. It is first recorded with this unit on 6 May 1940 and was then damaged in an accident on 7 November 1943 when it suffered 25 per cent damage at Heichling with Unteroffizier Alfons Schmidt injured.

Opposite above: This Ju 52/3m coded TB+BS was photographed at Neudorf-Oppeln in 1941. It was recorded as being with Flugzeugführerschule (C) 9 in February 1941, then Aufklärungsschule 1 Grossenhain April to July 1941 and finally Flugzeugführerschule (C) 4 from September 1941 to May 1944.

Opposite below: A training sortie for Ju 86s of I./Kampfgeschwader 253, winter 1937–8. Code on the nearest aircraft reads 33+111.

An unidentified Ju 52; in the background is a W34 with the code WL-OMW which would date the photo as being taken between January and October 1939.

3
RJ

DA AU

An unidentified Ju 86 E accident at Prague-Ruzyne, 1941.

Opposite above: A Ju 86 E-2, RJ+NV of Flugzeugführerschule (C) 18, Lüben, July 1943.

Opposite below: A Ju 86 E-2 DA+AU of Flugzeugführerschule (C) 12 which has suffered an accident at Prague-Ruzyne, 12 May 1941. This aircraft later flew with Flugzeugführerschule (B) 32.

Opposite above: An earlier accident at Prague-Ruzyne befell this Ju 86 E-1 of Flugzeugführerschule (C) 12 on 21 September 1940.

Opposite below: This is werk nummer 4018 and the crash occurred at 2045hrs 1km south of the airfield. The pilot, Fähnrich Friedrich Schulte, was injured.

Ju 86 E BQ+ND of Flugzeugführerschule (B) 3 after suffering an accident at Prague-Ruzyne in June 1941.

Opposite: Close-up of the Stuka's engine at Graz, 1938.

Working on a Ju 87 B of I./Stukageschwader 168. This photograph was taken in 1938 at Graz in Austria.

KJ UH

Above: VA+EV werk nummer 2075 was originally an A-1, being repaired by Arado in June 1940 emerging as a Ju 88 A-5 and finally being converted to a Ju 88 A-7 dual-seat trainer. Here it is a Ju 88 A-5 of Flugzeugführerschule (C)8 based at Wiener-Neustadt. Just visible is the unit shield which is a four-leaf clover.

Opposite above: A Stuka believed to have been from II./Stukaschule 2 which was based at Graz-Thalerhof in Austria in 1941–2.

Opposite below: Ju 88 A-4 werk nummer 6583 KJ+UH of Flugzeugführerschule (C) 14, Prague-Gbell. This aircraft also served with 9./Kampfgeschwader 1 and suffered 20 per cent damaged in an air attack on Sechschinskaja on 16 August 1943.

Flugzeugführerschule (C) 8, Wiener-Neustadt. The nearest Ju 88 A-5 is coded TB+LD werk nummer 7101. In the background is Ju 88 A-5 werk nummer 6039 NF+HL which was eventually converted to an A-7 and involved in an accident in 1944. Note that the last two letters of both aircraft are in white.

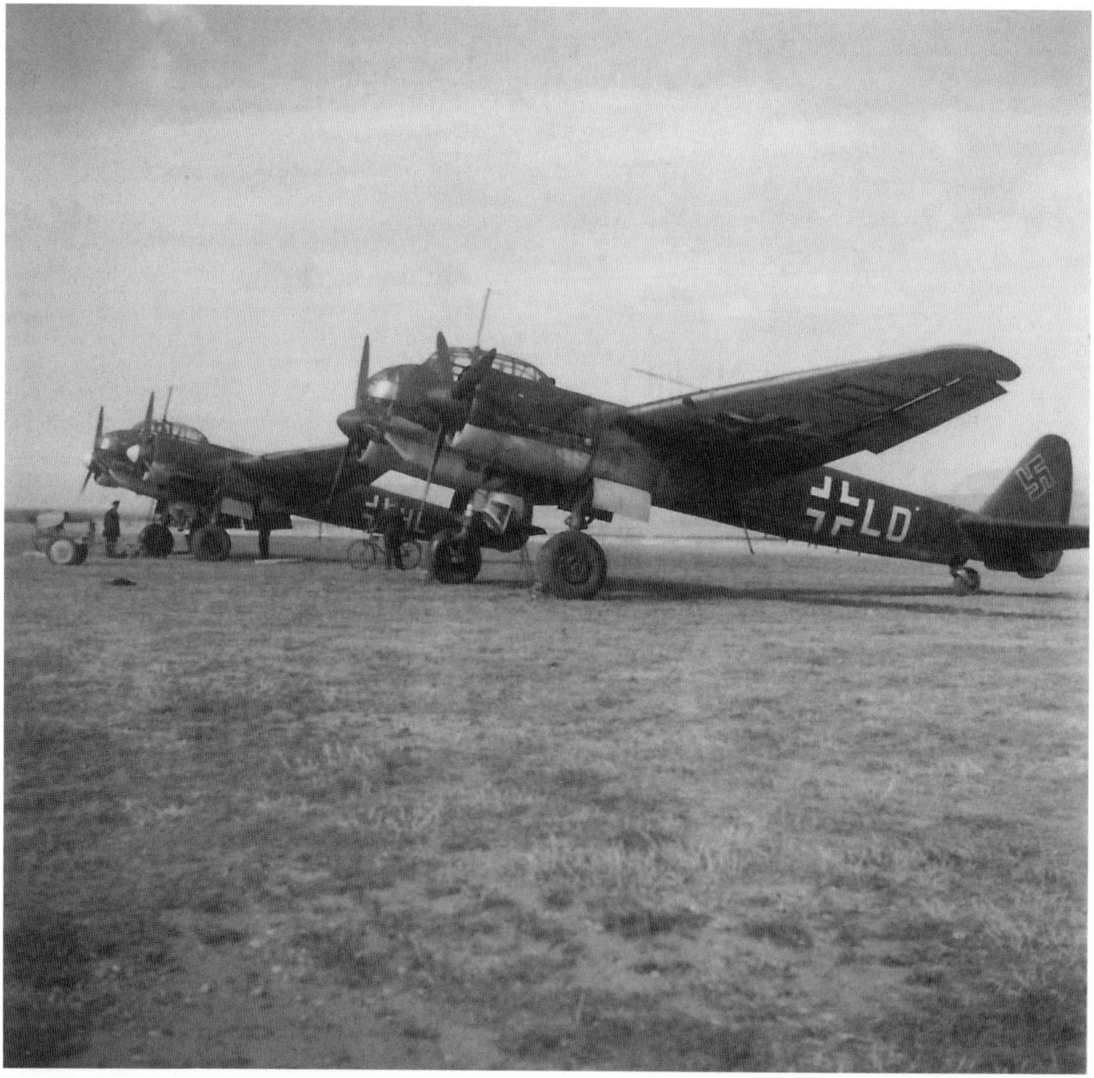

A clear shot of the Flugzeugführerschule (C) 8 badge – white shield and green clover-leaf on a Ju 88 A-7.

A Ju 88 A-7 (possibly A-12) of Flugzeugführerschule (C) 18, Schönfeld-Seifersdorf. This photo was taken in July 1943 and shows an Unteroffizier Uhlig. The badge is a shield divided diagonally into gold and blue with a black eagle's head top right.

Ju 88 A-5s of Flugzeugführerschule (C) 14 at Prague-Gbell, 1942. Although not visible, this school's badge was a black cartoon raven carrying the letter C on a yellow disc.

Sturz 9

The photographer was posted to III./Kampfgeschwader 30 in mid-1941. Ergänzungs Kampfgeschwader 5 would be disbanded in May 1941 at the time that IV (Ergänzungs) Gruppe were forming in each Kampfgeschwader.

Opposite above: A Ju 88 A-5 of Flugzeugführerschule (C) 14, Prague-Gbell.

Opposite below: Ju 88 A-1, werk nummer 7146 DH+AJ of Ergänzungs Kampfgeschwader 5 which was based at Barth. This aircraft crashed near Libbenzig, Neusalz/Elbe at 2250 hrs on 10 April 1941.

Opposite above: The white band indicates the Mediterranean theatre and the only crew names are Oberfeldwebel Hoffmann (Fluzeugführer) and Unteroffizier Thalhammer (Bordfunker), who with the other two crew were uninjured.

Opposite below: A Ju 88 A- of IV./Kampfgeschwader 77 practising anti-shipping missions, Danzig Bay, 1942.

This is believed to be Ju 88 A-5, werk nummer 3303 coded 3Z+HV of IV./Kampfgeschwader 77 which has come to grief in a vineyard near Bourges, France at 1445hrs on 2 October 1942.

The unit initially responsible for anti-shipping training was Kampfschulegeschwader 2 which was formed at Grossenbrode late 1941 under the leadership of Oberst Karl Stockmann after which it moved to Grosseto in Italy. In March 1943 it became Kampfgeschwader 102. These Ju 88 A-4 LTs, the furthest being coded A8+BN of 5 Staffel, were part of Major Wilhelm Emond's II Gruppe.

Opposite above: The aircraft has a theatre band, presumably white, as IV./Kampfgeschwader 77, at this time commanded by Hauptmann Hans-Jörg Leuze, was based at Bourges, France.

Opposite below: In the summer of 1943, I./Kampfgeschwader 77, commanded by Major Willi Sölter, was withdrawn from the Mediterranean to Pillau in the Baltic. It there went from being a conventional bomber Gruppe to one that dropped torpedoes. It did not return to operations until the end of March 1944.

Opposite above: IV./Kampfgeschwader 40 based at Chateaudun converted pilots onto the Ju 88 C-6 (as well as Fw 200s) and subsequent posting to V./Kampfgeschwader 40. This Ju 88 C-6, coded F8+CU, is photographed between March and mid-April 1943 and appears to have kill markings on its tail indicating it had served operationally with V./Kampfgeschwader 40.

Opposite below: An unidentified Ju 88 from a training unit. The oversized numerals are usual on later training-school aircraft.

Just visible on the nose of this Ju 88 is werk nummer 6019 which identifies it as a Ju 88 A-7 dual trainer. This aircraft was coded CA+EM and is at Flugzeugführerschule C6 based at Kolberg. This aircraft was photographed by Leutnant Knud Gmelin probably on 19 November 1942. Gmelin would be posted to IV./Kampfgeschwader 40 at Chateaudun, France in March 1943 after which he joined V./Kampfgeschwader 40. He would be killed in action in June 1944.

38

Loading practice bombs to a Ju 88 of I./Kampfschulegeschwader 3 at Cognac, late 1942.

Bombs loaded, this I./Kampfschulegeschwader 3 Ju 88 is ready for a training sortie, Cognac, late 1942.

This I./Kampfschulegeschwader 3 aircraft has just one 250kg bomb loaded.

I./ Kampfschulegeschwader training sortie, south-west France 1942.

III./Kampfgeschwader 101 was formed from I./Kampfschulegeschwader 3 in February 1943 and only consisted of a Stab, 8 and 9 Staffeln.

Six aircraft of I./Kampfschulegeschwader 3 in formation over western France, 1942–3.

Opposite above: All three I./Kampfschulegeschwader 3 aircraft have the white fuselage band in different positions.

Opposite below: Believed to be V3+DK of 2./Kampfschulegeschwader 3.

A mixture of I./Kampfschulegeschwader 3 Ju 88s coded V3+DK, V32+HL and V3+EL. Note +HL has the letter 'h' on the tail.

Believed to be V3+GH of 1./Kampfschulegeschwader 3, again with the crude 'g' on the tail.

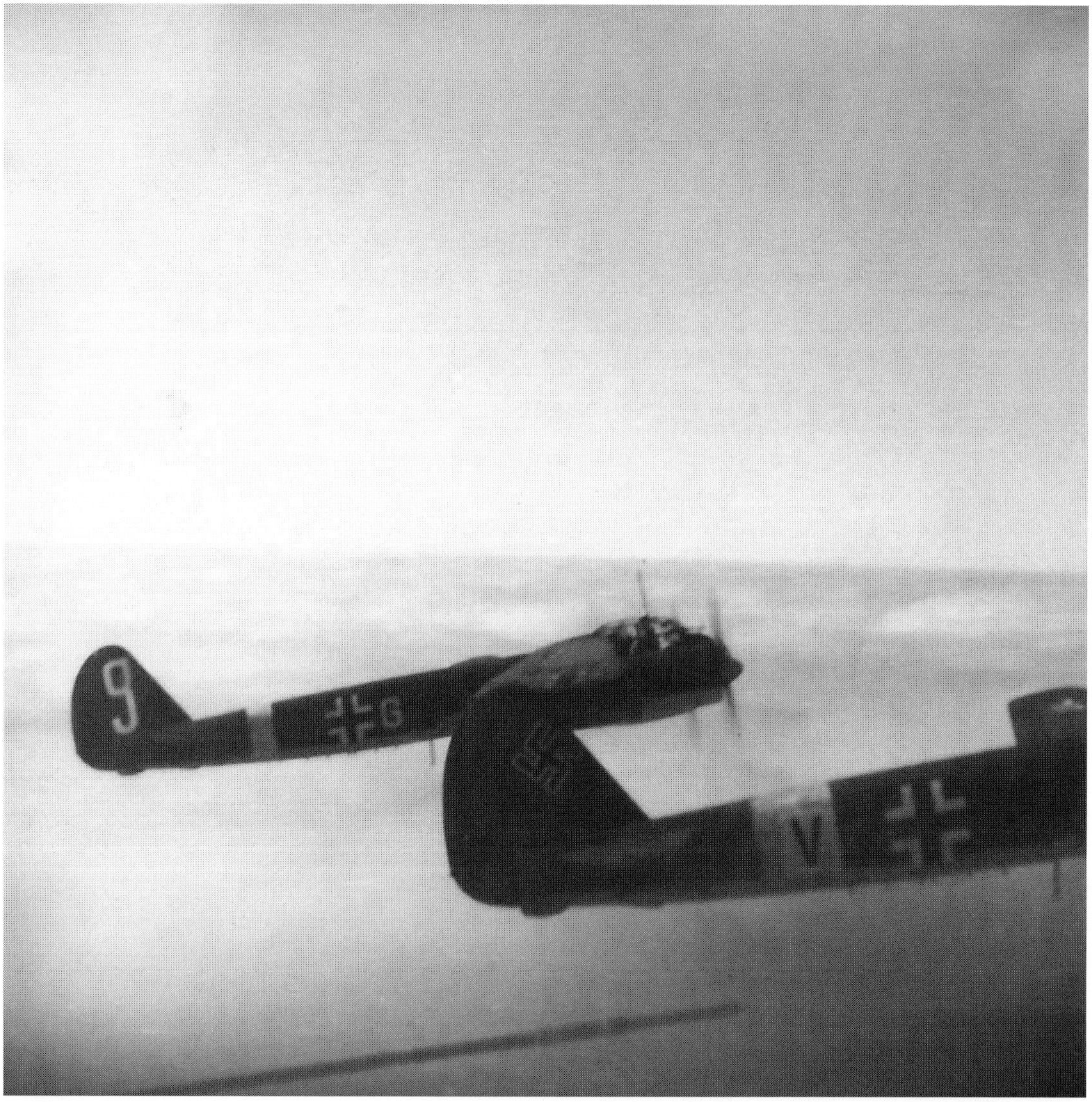

V3+DK getting even closer.

Looking down on a 2./Kampfschulegeschwader 3 Ju 88.

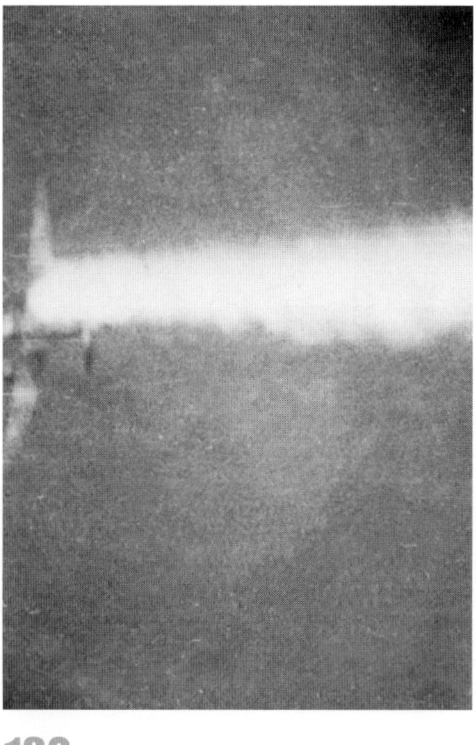

Ju 88 A-14 werk nummer 4102. 2./Kampfschulegruppe 3 became 3./Kampfgeschwader 101 in February 1943 and moved to Greifswald in June 1943. This aircraft was lost in an accident at Greifswald on 1 December 1943 with the deaths of Unteroffizier Peter Eschbacher (Fluezeugführer), Obergefreiter Anton Bolgk (Beobatcher), Unteroffizier Herbert Luschnigg (Bordfunker) and Obergefreiter Heinrich von Stein (Bordschütze). The badge is believed to be that of I./Kampfgeschwader 101 and has not been positively identified.

Last moments of a Ju 88 A-14 werk nummer 144105 U5+CV of 11./Kampfgeschwader 2 on 5 October 1943.

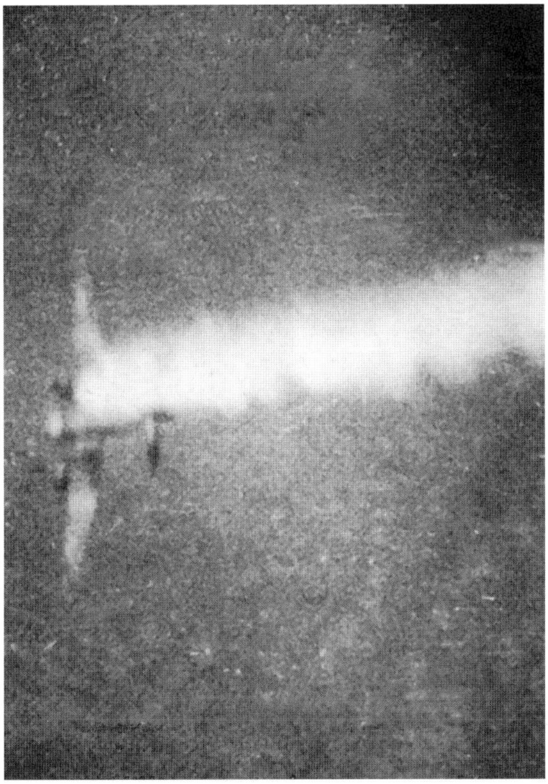

Above left: Unteroffizier Rudolf Möckel had just taken off from Villaroche in France on a technical/ training flight.

Above right: The Ju 88 was intercepted by Flying Officer Artie Ross and Pilot Officer 'Pinkie' Stark in Typhoons of 609 Squadron.

Right: The bomber crashed into a wood near Sevry and burst into flames. Although one of the crew baled out, Möckel, Gefreiter Alois Mocez (Beobachter), Unteroffizier Siegfried Zeidler (Bordfunker) and Obergefreiter Rudolf Tesky (Bordschütze) were all killed.

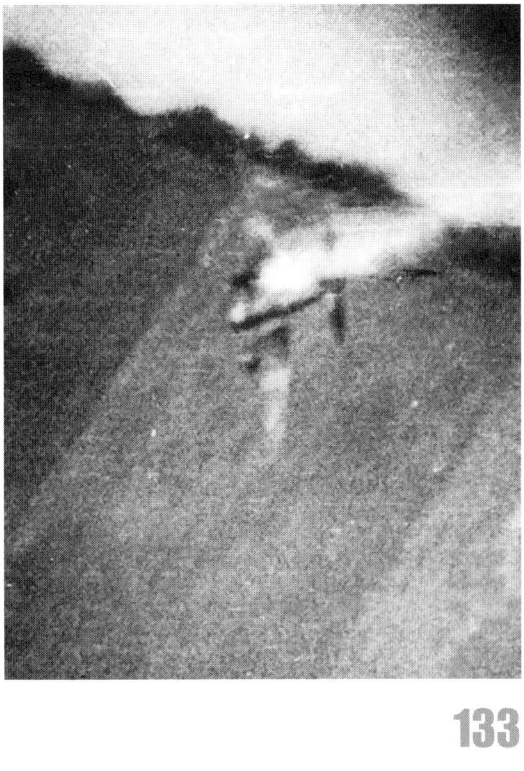

MESSERSCHMITT

Seen in pre-war civilian markings, the Bf 108 was a popular and successful aircraft before, during and after the war.

This Bf 108 B served with Stab./Kampfgeschwader 53 as a communications and training aircraft. It was later reported with 1./Jagdgeschwader Süd at Nimes between 24 April and 9 June 1943.

Bf 108 B TL+AB performed similar duties for Kampfgeschwader 100 in 1940; its eventual fate is not known.

Preparing a Bf 110 C for a training sortie; the date, location or unit is not known.

Opposite above: This is Bf 110D-3 werk nummer 3696 CC+MZ flown by 1./Nachtjagdschule 1 during autumn 1941.The third letter of the stammkennzeichen has been removed and the last letter over painted with a white 11.

Opposite below: A Bf 110 G-2 of an unidentified training unit. It appears to have a unit emblem below the cockpit.

Opposite above: Three Bf 110s from 1./Nachtjagdgeschule 1. The furthest aircraft have training unit numerals painted on them while the nearest just has the stammkennzeichen which identifies it as a C-1 variant werk nummer 1798 which was with 1./Nachtjagdgeschwader 1 in 1940 and lost in an accident on 27 May 1943 with II./Schlachtgeschwader 101.

Opposite below: An Me 163 rocket fighter getting airborne on a test or training flight.

Crew training with the Me 321 glider, possibly from I./Kampfgeschwader zbV 323. The Bf 110 in this unit was used for towing the massive glider.

One of the first prototype Me 163s getting airborne.

Kampfgeschwader 6 was a Ju 88/188 bomber unit but in 1944 was retrained on the Me 262. This shows an Me 262 of III./Kampfgeschwader (J) 6 at Prague-Ruszyn, March 1945.

White 11 of Kampfgeschwader (J) 6 at Prague-Ruszyn in April 1945. The unit never completed its training.

Kampfgeschwader (J) 6 at Prague-Ruszyn in April 1945; too little too late.

MESSERSCHMITT BF 109

A Bf 109 D of II.(S)/Jagdgeschwader 134 which in November 1938 became II./Jagdgeschwader 142. This unit would then become II./Zerstörergeschwader 142 in January 1939 and in May 1939 would become II/Zerstörergeschwader 26. It would then convert from the Bf 109 D to the Bf 110 until early 1940 and the Bf 109s were then assigned to training or withdrawn from service.

This is Bf 109 B-1 werk nummer 1032 coded TC+KB which first flew on 18 August 1937 with the civilian code D-ISJE. It is thought it was used for development of the Bf 109 F wing but it is believed that this photograph was taken in 1940–1 at Jagdfliegerschule 1 Werneuchen.

TC+KB was badly damaged in an accident at Prenzlau on 5 April 1943 whilst with the Überprüfungsschule (für) Erweiterter Luftwaffen-Führerschein (Examination School for Air Force Advanced Flying Certificate). It was subsequently written off.

Opposite above: A Bf 109 B of Jagdfliegerschule 5 being started by means of an inertia starter at Wien-Schwechat, autumn/early winter 1940. Note the camera underneath the wing.

Opposite below: Bf 109 B of Jagdfliegerschule 5 over the Austrian countryside, October–November 1940. The number 9 lies within a yellow fuselage band.

Fähnrich Leopold Wenger getting into the cockpit of his Bf 109 B/D at Jagdfliegerschule 5, Wien-Schwechat, October–November 1940. The badge on the nose appears to be a hand similar to that of 1./Jagdgeschwader 102, a Bf 109 unit which in January 1940 became a Bf 110 unit. The badge of Jagdfliegerschule 5 was a blue, white and yellow shield incorporating a Bf 109.

NO EZ

Second from right is Oberfeldwebel Franz Gawlik. An experienced fighter pilot, he flew with 2./Jagdgeschwader 53 before becoming an instructor with Hauptmann Dr Rudolf Lüder's 2.Ergänzungs/Jagdgeschwader 53 based at St Jean D'Angély in western France where this photo was taken. He managed to score his fifth kill of the war, a Halifax, on 24 July 1941 and would survive the war.

Opposite above: ND+EZ was a Bf 109 D werk nummer 420. Its last unit before being removed from service was Luftdienst Kommando 1/11; its previous and subsequent service history is unknown.

Opposite below: Either a Bf 109 E-4/N or Bf 109 E-7 fitted with a 300-litre centre-line tank. The aircraft appears to be very new and still retains the factory codes, the last letter of which was F. It is possible that this aircraft was photographed at Wien-Schwechat in late 1940.

Opposite above: This Bf 109 F-2 probably belongs to Ergänzungs Jagdgruppe-Süd which was one of three fighter pools formed in 1942 as the pilot who took the photograph, Uffz Werner Schammert, joined 10./Jagdgeschwader 26 in the latter half of 1942 from this unit. Note the numerals painted just below the cockpit indicating that this is a training aircraft.

Opposite below: There is a mix of training aircraft behind this Bf 109 F-2 which appears to be coded PD+O.

I./Jagdgeschwader 1 became III./Jagdgeschwader 27 at the start of the Battle of Britain and carried numerals on the nose but no markings fore and aft of the fuselage cross, the practice being discontinued when III./Jagdgeschwader 27 converted to the Bf 109 F in 1941. It is also possible that these Bf 109 Es are serving with Ergänzungs/Jagdgeschwader 27 which was formed in November 1940 at Oldenburg and would be commanded for much of its existence by Hauptmann Herbert Nebenführ.

Bf 109 B-1 TC+KB, showing that the letters KB are much larger that the letters TC.

Opposite above: Bf 109 F of 3./Jagdfliegerschule 4 (later Jagdgeschwader 104) photographed at Fürth in 1943.

Opposite below: Bf 109 B-1 werk nummer 1032 TC+KB photographed by Leutnant Siegfried Storsberg at Jagdfliegerschule 1 Werneuchen in 1940–1. Note the camera under the port wing.

Opposite above: Bf 109B-1 werk nummer 392 NF+LQ was with Jagdfliegerschule 2 and crashed near Magdeburg on 18 September 1940, killing its pilot. It is therefore possible that NF+LR was with the same unit.

Opposite below: Bf 109 B-1 werk nummer 1032 TC+KB, framed by the door of the watch hut.

Bf 109 B-1 NF+LR at either Jagdfliegerschule 1 Werneuchen or Jagdfliegerschule 2 Schleissheim, 1940.

A Bf 109 B at Jagdfliegerschule 1 at Werneuchen, 1939. Note the camera under the port wing root. The pilot is Leutnant Franz Fiby who would join 3./Jagdgeschwader 2 later that year. He would survive the war.

Opposite: Bf 109 Es of the Ergänzungsgruppe/Jagdgeschwader 53 at St Jean D'Angély in 1941. Consisting two Staffel, 1 Staffel was the operational Staffel and 2 Staffel the training Staffel. Spinner and cowlings are yellow and the white numerals could possibly indicate 2 Staffel aircraft as 1 Staffel had black numerals.

MISCELLANEOUS

Practice bombs ready for use at II./Stukaschule 2, Graz, 1941.

Produced by someone undergoing training is this risqué cartoon 'Is there much draught in the plane, Herr Pilot?' 'Well it depends, Madam'.

Opposite above: Photographed at Luftkriegsschule 4 by another pilot, this would prove that it is Caudron C.445 BC+QF.

Opposite below: Seen at Flugzeugführerschule (C) 18 at Schönfeld-Seifersdorf in June 1943 is this Caudron C.445 werk nummer 800 SF+DN. In July 1943, it went to Luftkriegsschule 3 and was destroyed in an air raid on Halberstadt on 30 May 1944.

Former French Air Force Caudron C445 seen with LKS42 at Fürstenfeldbruck. First letters are BC which could indicate it to be BC+QF werk nummer 430/9158 which was at Luftkriegsschule 4 from December 1941 but also flew with Flugzeugführerschule (A) 61.

Opposite above: In addition to powered training, there was also glider training. This is a DFS 230 with the werk nummer 156, taken in 1941.

Opposite below: This captured Dutch Fokker G1B was given the Stammkennzeichen DE+OO and is seen here with Flugzeugführerschule (C) 8 at Weiner-Neustadt.

This Dewoitine D.5 20 was photographed with 1./Jagdgeschwader 105 at Chartres, 1944.

456

Opposite above: An aircraft made popular by former First World War ace Ernst Udet was this Curtiss Hawk II, seen at Hannover in 1936. However, it was not adopted wholesale by the Luftwaffe.

Opposite below: An unusual acquisition was this Czech Letov S328 GA+AK which was recorded at Schule/Fliegerausbildungsregiment 13 in July 1941.

This Deutscher Luftsportverband DFS 'Kranich' (or crane) glider was photographed at Neudorf, 1940.

GA

This captured NA 64 is being operated by Flugzeugführerschule (A/B) 116 at Neudorf-Oppeln, 1941.

PEOPLE

Seen at Achmer in 1941 whilst converting from the Do 17 to the Do 217 with 10./Kampfgeschwader 2 are this crew (left to right): Unteroffizier Ernst Geselle (+ 22 April 1942), Leutnant Karl von Manowarda (POW 15 May 1944), Feldwebel Rudolf Leitgebel and Unteroffizier Heinrich Kaiser (+ 15 May 1944).

Above: Trainee aircrew with Fliegerausbildungsregiment 42, Salzwedel, 1939.

Opposite above: Having just completed training with Jagdfliegerschule Werneuchen, these pilots have just been posted to III./Jagdgeschwader 132. (Left to right) Leutnant Rudolf Heymann, Leutnant Heinz Holborn, Leutnant Hans-Ulrich Kettling, ?, ?, Gefreiter Erich Zickler.

Opposite below: Gunners training with an MG 15 with the Hs 126 unit (H)/13, March 1940.

Opposite above: Gunnery training with 3./Kampfgeschwader 30, 1944.

Opposite below: Dinghy training at Flugzeugführerschule (C) 14, Prague-Gbell. This came in useful for the man on the left, Oberfähnrich Ulrich Laubis, who was shot down into the Channel in June 1944 and taken prisoner.

More gunnery training, this time with Fliegerschützenschule 4, Graudenz, 1940–1.

PN

Ground school was essential for new aircrew; here trainees are being watched by their instructors.

Opposite above: On the right is Obergefreiter Hans Weinberger. On completion of training, he was posted to 2./Stukageschwader 77 but was then killed together with Unteroffizier Karl-Heinz Fründt flying a Ju 87 D-5, werk nummer 142081 V8+OB of 1./Nachtschlachtgruppe 1 which crashed near Breitscheid on 23 December 1944.

Opposite below: Trainee fighter pilots being taught how to attack enemy aircraft by an experienced pilot.

Opposite: Trainees at the Flugzeugführerschule A/B 43, Crailsheim. On the left is Eugen Marggraf who would be shot down in March 1944 flying with 1 Staffel (Fern)/ Aufklärungsgruppe 120 during a reconnaissance fight over the Shetland Islands; he and two of his crew were captured, the fourth would be killed.

An experienced Oberleutnant (who is wearing the Frontflugspange [mission clasp] having flown a number of operational flights) teaches pilots from Jagdgeschwader 302 how to attack a formation of B-17s.

Opposite above: Jagdfliegerschule Schleissheim, September–December 1939. All would be in combat very shortly: many of them would not survive 1940.

Opposite below: Three friends during final training at Jagdfliegerschule Schleissheim, December 1939. All three would be posted to Jagdgeschwader 2. Left to right: Wilfried Reinwald would be injured in an accident on 27 April 1940 with 4./Jagdgeschwader 2 and did not return to flying until 1941. He would survive the war with six victories. Julius Meimberg would join 4./Jagdgeschwader 2 in December 1939. He would shoot down fifty-three aircraft, be awarded the Knight's Cross and survived the war but would be wounded a number of times. Egon Mayer would join 3./Jagdgeschwader 2 in December 1939; he would shoot down 102 aircraft, be awarded the Knight's Cross with Oak Leaves and Swords but would be killed in action on 2 March 1944.

More dinghy training – this time for crews from I./Kampfgeschwader 4, spring 1940.

VARIOUS

Opposite above: Another mixture seen at Fliegerausbildungsregiment 13, Pilsen, April–May 1940. CA+UO is a Go 145 A which was then with Fliegerausbildungsregiment 32 in February 1941 and Luftkriegsschule 2 in September 1944. DA+NX is a He 72 B Kadett which was then with Fliegerausbildungsregiment 24 from September 1940.

Opposite below: This airfield houses a Fi 156 Storch, what appears to be a Klemm 35 and a He 111 of Kampfgeschwader 53. Note the stammkennzeichen is on the upper surfaces of the wing of both the Klemm and Storch.

Below: Photographed at Grosse Kampffliegerschule 1 Hörsching is a mixture of aircraft – Do 17 E or F, Do 17 Z and a Ju 86 behind.

Opposite above: This photo, taken at Schleswig in 1939, uses a Ar 66 (WL-LMU) and Go 145 (WL- IUXA) as a backdrop. Schleswig was the home of Fliegerausbildungsregiment 16.

Opposite below: Despite the snow, training is continuing at this school; eight aircraft can be seen.

A Do 23 with the pre-war codes whilst what appears to be a Klemm 31 has the WL codes which dates this photo to between January and October 1939.

WL-I LMU

Five Go 145s and a single Fw 44 are at this airfield.